IT'S TIME TO EAT PASSION FRUIT

It's Time to Eat PASSION FRUIT

Walter the Educator

Silent King Books
A WhichHead Entertainment Imprint

Copyright © 2024 by Walter the Educator

All rights reserved. No part of this book may be reproduced in any manner whatsoever without written per- mission except in the case of brief quotations embodied in critical articles and reviews.

First Printing, 2024

Disclaimer

This book is a literary work; the story is not about specific persons, locations, situations, and/or circumstances unless mentioned in a historical context. Any resemblance to real persons, locations, situations, and/or circumstances is coincidental. This book is for entertainment and informational purposes only. The author and publisher offer this information without warranties expressed or implied. No matter the grounds, neither the author nor the publisher will be accountable for any losses, injuries, or other damages caused by the reader's use of this book. The use of this book acknowledges an understanding and acceptance of this disclaimer.

It's Time to Eat PASSION FRUIT is a collectible early learning book by Walter the Educator suitable for all ages belonging to Walter the Educator's Time to Eat Book Series. Collect more books at WaltertheEducator.com

USE THE EXTRA SPACE TO TAKE NOTES AND DOCUMENT YOUR MEMORIES

PASSION FRUIT

It's time to eat, come gather 'round,

It's Time to Eat

Passion Fruit

A special fruit that can be found.

Purple, yellow, smooth, or rough,

Passion fruit is yummy stuff!

Crack it open, what's inside?

Golden juice and seeds that hide.

Little treasures, tart and sweet,

A tropical snack that's fun to eat!

Scoop it out with a little spoon,

It smells like flowers in full bloom.

Its tangy taste will make you smile,

A treat that's worth each little while.

It's full of goodness, fresh and bright,

A burst of sunshine, pure delight.

It helps us grow, both big and strong,

With every bite, you can't go wrong.

It's Time to Eat

Passion Fruit

Mix it up in a smoothie blend,

Or share it with your fruity friends.

Pour it on yogurt, make a juice,

Passion fruit's magic has so much use!

Its seeds go crunch, its juice goes zing,

It's like a party that makes you sing.

Close your eyes and take a bite,

Feel the flavors take flight!

Passion fruit comes from far away,

It brings us joy every day.

From sunny lands where it grows best,

This fruit's a gift, we feel so blessed.

It's great for breakfast, lunch, or snack,

A healthy choice that keeps on track.

Enjoy it fresh, or in a dish,

It's Time to Eat
Passion Fruit

It's like a hug with every wish!

So let's all shout, "Hooray, hooray!"

For passion fruit on our snack tray.

A healthy snack we'll always choose,

With passion fruit, you cannot lose!

It's time to eat, come take your seat,

This tasty fruit can't be beat.

Passion fruit, so pure and fine,

It's Time to Eat
Passion Fruit

A little treat that's simply divine!

ABOUT THE CREATOR

Walter the Educator is one of the pseudonyms for Walter Anderson. Formally educated in Chemistry, Business, and Education, he is an educator, an author, a diverse entrepreneur, and he is the son of a disabled war veteran. "Walter the Educator" shares his time between educating and creating. He holds interests and owns several creative projects that entertain, enlighten, enhance, and educate, hoping to inspire and motivate you. Follow, find new works, and stay up to date with Walter the Educator™

at WaltertheEducator.com

www.ingramcontent.com/pod-product-compliance
Lightning Source LLC
LaVergne TN
LVHW052013060526
838201LV00059B/4018